51 Ways to Entertain Your Housecat While You're Out

**Easy-to-Make Toys & Games Guaranteed
to Keep Your Pet Busy and Happy**

Stephanie Laland

BARNES
&NOBLE
B O O K S
NEW YORK

2002 Barnes & Noble Books

ISBN 0-7607-3191-8

Printed and bound in the United States of America

02 03 04 05 06 MC 9 8 7 6 5 4 3 2 1

FG

Please send any ideas you have for toys and games, as well as stories and quotes, to the author in care of Avon Books for possible inclusion in the author's next book. Be sure to include the name of your cat so Stephanie Laland can mention him or her. First cats to write get the credit!

"The smallest feline is a masterpiece."

*—Leonardo da Vinci;
from his Notebooks*

Introduction

What do you see when you come home from work?

- Shredded draperies?
- Your favorite chair in shambles?
- The toilet paper unraveled throughout your home?
- Your important papers scattered all over the floor and perhaps nibbled at the corners?
- Or even worse: Is your place neat as a pin while your kitty looks bored and listless, getting rounder in the middle because he's had nothing to do all day and his only interest in life is the food bowl?

The solution to all these problems and more is easier than you might think.

Cats in the wild had to capture their food, and the hunt was a thrill that gave them the exercise and stimulation they needed. Their world was exhilarating and full of new smells and stimuli that kept them on their toes and their senses alert.

So if your kitty is getting too round and looks bored stiff, don't blame the cat. Create an environment in your own home—even if it's just a small apartment—that will be fun and interesting for your cat.

Which cats need this book?

- apartment cats
- cats of the elderly
- cats temporarily kept indoors because of ailments
- cats who live in the country and cannot go out for fear of coyotes or other predators
- cats confined until they can be spayed or neutered

- young cats and kittens
- cats new to their household, confined until they get their shots
- cats kept indoors because they live in areas where feline AIDS or feline leukemia are prevalent
- cats living with people who may not want or be able to play with them frequently
- cats whose wise human companions realize that indoor cats live longer than outdoor cats

Human beings struck a deal with felines ages ago when we domesticated them. They were to give us companionship and keep mice away, and we were to give them companionship and provide a comfortable environment. This book will answer all your questions about how to do just that, as well as provide fascinating stories, poems, quotations, and helpful hints to make life with the most popular pet in the world more fun for both of you.

Have fun!

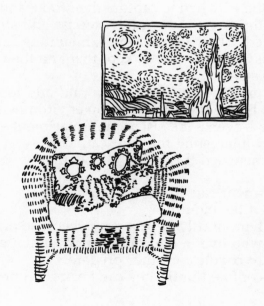

51 Ways to Entertain
Your Housecat
While You're Out

 # BOUNCING BATTER

Cats love to bat at something that bounces back. Attach a weight (such as an empty vitamin jar filled with beans) securely to one end of a stick (duct tape works well). On the other end of the stick, fasten a string attached to a dangling toy. Attach another string at the center of the stick so you can hang the Bouncing Batter from a hook installed over a doorway. The weighted end makes the toy bobble up and down when the cat bats at it. To determine the right height at which to suspend the toy, play with your cat by hand-holding the stick before hanging the Bouncing Batter. Make sure the string with the toy attached is long enough so your cat doesn't get hit by the weight.

Remember, cats can hurt themselves by getting tangled in string or swallowing it. To prevent mishaps, run the string through a two-foot piece of plastic tubing from your hardware store. Tie a big knot in the string so the tubing can't ride up.

"It is axiomatic that you cannot order a cat to play. You can only coax and beguile."
—SYDNEY

SCRATCH AND CATCH

Put a few walnuts (still in their shells, of course) in an empty tissue box and tape over the opening. Cut a paw-sized hole in the side of the box (big enough for a cat to get the nuts out) and rattle the box in front of your cat. Cats love to try to scratch small objects out of tight openings—it challenges their mouse-catching abilities. The sound of nuts still rattling in the box intrigues them. Your cat may spend hours trying to get all the nuts out.

*"If a man could be crossed with the cat,
it would improve the man
but deteriorate the cat."*
—MARK TWAIN

EXPLORER KITTY

Just as you enjoy changes in your environment and new places to see and explore, so does your cat. Even if she already has her own hideaway, staring at the same old walls can become tiresome. In just fifteen minutes, you can construct a new environment for your kitty to explore. Cut up a few old boxes, add holes, tunnels, and peep-holes, and tape it all together. Put toys inside, too. There is nothing like a new place to explore to make a happy cat.

THE BAD KITTENS
(to be read aloud to your cat)

You may call, you may call,
But the little black cats won't hear you.
The little black cats are maddened
By the bright green light of the moon.
They are whirling and running and hiding
They are wild who were once so confiding
They are crazed when the moon is riding—
You will not catch the kittens soon.
They care not for saucers of milk
They think not of pillows of silk.
Your softest crooningest call
Is less than the buzzing of flies.
They are seeing more than you see
They are hearing more than you hear
And out of the darkness they peer
With a goblin light in their eyes.
—ELIZABETH J. COATSWORTH

LORD OF THE JUNGLE

An indoor kitty can pretend he is still lord of the jungle if you grow some of his favorite plants in a box where he can sit. It's even better if your cat can look out a window from his jungle.

Some safe plants for cats to chew are: Swedish ivy, coleus, ferns, spider plants, and palms. Check others before you purchase them because many plants, such as poinsettia, are quite poisonous. Some other plants poisonous to kitties are azaleas, chrysanthemums, holly, ivy, mistletoe, philodendron, dieffenbachia, and wisteria.

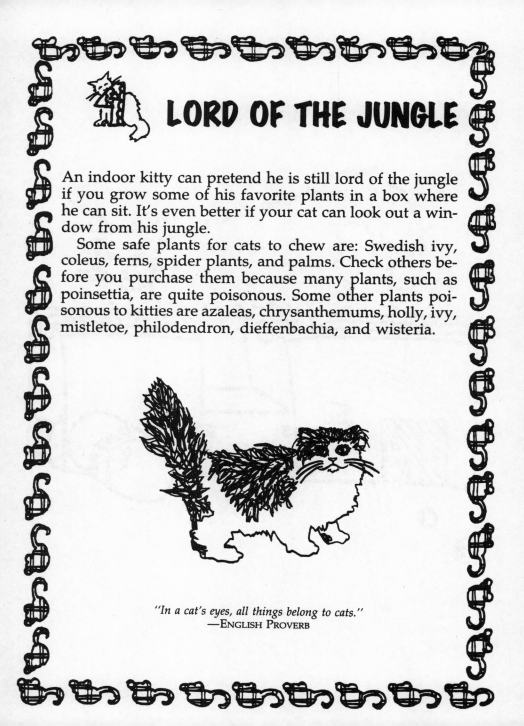

"In a cat's eyes, all things belong to cats."
—ENGLISH PROVERB

5 I REMEMBER MAMA

For an insecure kitten that cries heartrendingly when you leave, make a tape recording of the kitten purring while you pet him. Then leave the purr tape playing next to kitty's favorite cushion when you leave. While recording, you can vary the purring sounds by holding the microphone sometimes by kitty's tummy and sometimes by his throat. The sound of purring near his own cushion or blankets will reassure the kitten and help him feel safe.

Al had a special way to leave a private message on Linda's answering machine. He would pet his cat while holding her in his lap by the receiver. When Linda came home and heard a loud purring on her answering machine she knew she should call Al.

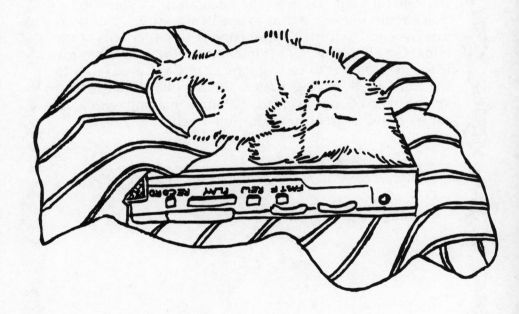

6 THE PAPER CHASE

Paper ribbon sold at craft and sewing shops makes an excellent toy. It is sold still twisted and costs only about ten cents a yard. To use it as decoration in your home, you should untwist it, but to use it as a kitty toy untwist just the ends to form a paper rope with paper fans at the ends. Cats love this. Use it in conjunction with other toy ideas by taping it to ceiling fans as in Cat Carousel or to the stick in Bouncing Batter. Or simply attach it to a spring over a doorway. And, of course, playing with your cat by hand is great fun with this lively toy!

SPARRING PARTNER

The Sparring Partner is a great toy much favored by cats. Attach any small toy to a spring about eight inches long. Thread the spring through an equal length of flexible plastic tubing. Drill a hole the exact diameter of the tubing through the middle of a twelve-inch length of two-by-twelve construction lumber. Fill the hole with epoxy and fit the end of the tube-covered spring into it. Cover the board with carpet.

The cat tries to bite the toy, which bobs away on its spring. My cats showed a marked preference for biting the spring part of the toy, which is why it's important to cover the spring with some protective flexible plastic or rubber tubing. Check periodically for signs of wear.

"Of all the toys available, none is better designed than the owner himself. A large multipurpose plaything, its parts can be made to move in almost any direction. It comes completely assembled and it makes a sound when you jump on it."
—STEPHEN BAKER

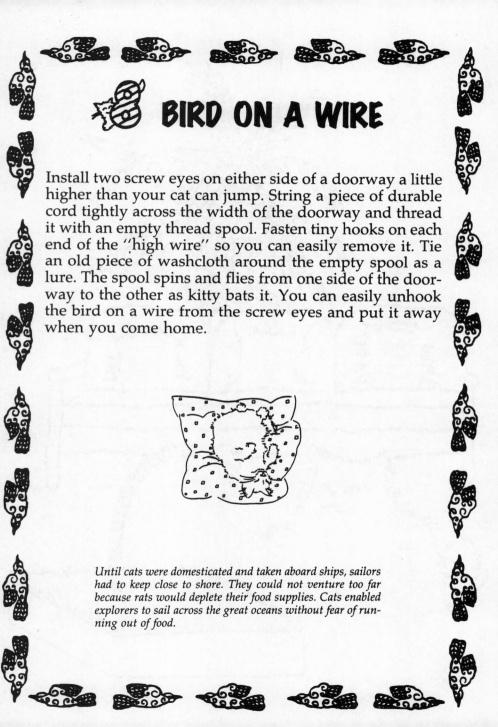

BIRD ON A WIRE

Install two screw eyes on either side of a doorway a little higher than your cat can jump. String a piece of durable cord tightly across the width of the doorway and thread it with an empty thread spool. Fasten tiny hooks on each end of the "high wire" so you can easily remove it. Tie an old piece of washcloth around the empty spool as a lure. The spool spins and flies from one side of the doorway to the other as kitty bats it. You can easily unhook the bird on a wire from the screw eyes and put it away when you come home.

Until cats were domesticated and taken aboard ships, sailors had to keep close to shore. They could not venture too far because rats would deplete their food supplies. Cats enabled explorers to sail across the great oceans without fear of running out of food.

TUNNELING

A tunnel exploratorium is an ideal toy for small apartments because it is mostly tucked away. Purchase a length of flexible ABS tubing large enough in diameter for your cat to crawl through. (Try a plumbing or construction supply store.) Put a few balls or catnip toys in the tunnel. Cats love to ferret things out; succeeding at this challenge makes them very proud. Place the flexible tube behind a sofa or around a chair.

Be sure to recycle the ABS tubing if your cat gets too big for it; you don't want to come home and find a stuck kitty.

"Honest as a cat when the cream is out of reach."
—Anonymous

 # 10 SNAKE

String several empty thread spools together with durable cord, leaving enough space between the spools so the snake can bend easily. Securely tie both ends. You can add bells between the spools or at the ends for extra excitement.

"The playful kitten, with its pretty little tigerish gambols, is infinitely more amusing than half the people one is obliged to live with in this world."
—LADY SYDNEY MORGAN

 # SPRAY CATNIP

To add extra interest to cat toys or scratching posts, try spray catnip. It is essence of catnip sold in aerosol cans at pet shops.

Be careful when you spray because your cat will also be attracted to wherever the spray goes. Put the toy on a newspaper before spraying, and then throw out the newspaper.

"When I hear someone say 'I hate cats,'
I don't frown on them or view them with disdain.
I simply recognize that they haven't had the opportunity
to be accepted and owned by a cat."
—WARREN AND FAY ECKSTEIN

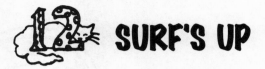

SURF'S UP

If you live near an ocean, you may be able to obtain an old wetsuit. Neoprene, cut into long, thin strips and hung from a doorframe can prove very enticing to cats. Neoprene strips have a springy, spongy quality.

EDUCATION

When People think that Kittens play,
It's really quite the other way.
For when they chase a Ball or Bobbin
They learn to catch a Mouse or Robin.

The Kitten, deaf to Duty's call,
Who will not chase the bouncing ball,
A hungry Cathood will enjoy,
The scorn of Mouse and Bird and Boy.
—OLIVER HERFORD

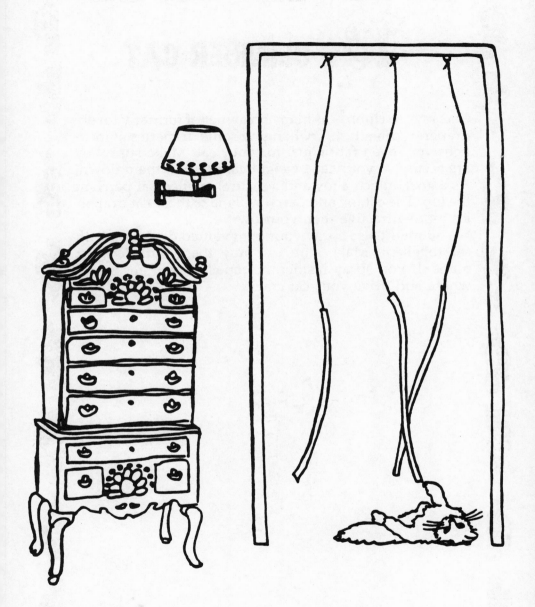

13 CLIMBER CAT

Cats love to climb—as many an owner of formerly lovely draperies can attest. Try hanging some draperies of inexpensive woven fabric just for your cat. Make sure they are secure so your cat's weight cannot pull them down. As a goal, attach a toy and a securely nailed cat perch at the top. The cat toy and perch will make these cat draperies more attractive than your own.

You might also spray your own valued draperies with cat repellent. Make sure to spray them outside your home. If you spray inside, the repellent will get everywhere and drive your cat crazy.

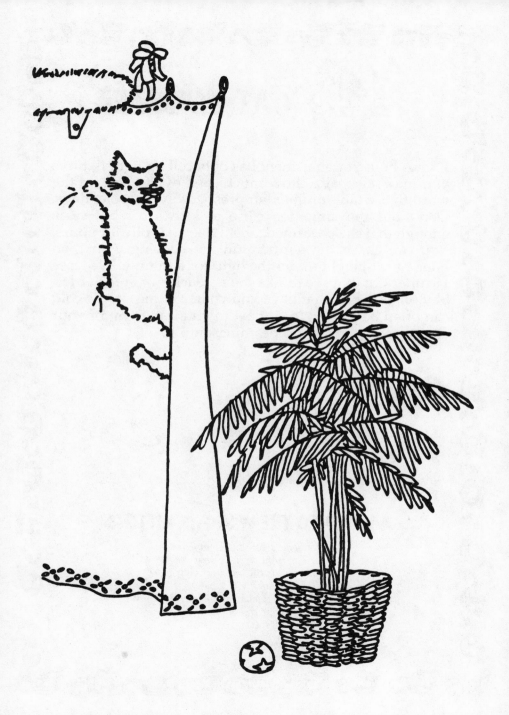

14 CAT WARMER

If your house or apartment has only ceiling light fixtures you may not realize how much cats love to bask in the warmth of a table or floor lamp, especially on cooler days. Don't put the lamp too close to kitty's fur but close enough that she's warmed. She'll sleep happily for hours. You can check the temperature by keeping your own hand at cat-height under the light for a minute. We tease Heather Cat that she thinks she's a packet of French fries. Shy or stray cats that have known hard times in the cold can often be coaxed to sit next to you if the arm of your chair has a warm lamp beaming onto it.

A WORD TO THE WISE FOR KITTENS

O fearsome tiger, big as my hand,
Take pity on your prey.
The hands that battle and bear your mark
Fetch herring and pâté.
The hand you claw and hackerel
Opens your can of mackerel.
—STEPHANIE LALAND

15 SNUGGLE SHELTER

Cover one side of a rectangular piece of cardboard with fake fur, roll it into a tube with the fur inside, and tape the ends together. Make the tube just cat sized for a snug fit to give kitty a safe private place that brings back warm memories of kittenhood. You can also line your cat's favorite cardboard box with fake fur and place it on its side.

"Nobody who is not prepared to spoil cats
will get from them the reward they are able to give
those who do spoil them."
—SIR COMPTON MACKENZIE

16 CAT CAROUSEL

If you are lucky enough to have a ceiling fan, you can make a cat carousel for your kitty. Attach long strips of newspaper to the blades with masking tape and leave the fan running at low speed. (Masking tape will come off the fan blades easily when kitty pulls on the newspaper strips.) Don't use string—cats can get tangled in it or swallow it, which can be dangerous if you're not home. Several strips of paper should be taped together until the strips are long enough to skim the ground when the fan is turned on. If your fan's blades turn too quickly, tape the paper strips closer to the center.

THE GAME

Watching a ball on the end of a string,
Watching it swing back and to,
Oh, I do think it the pleasantest thing
Ever a Kitten can do.

First it goes this way, then it goes that,
Just like a bird on the wing.
And all of a tremble I crouch on the mat
Like a Lion, preparing to spring.

And now with a terrible deafening mew,
Like a Tiger I leap on my prey,
And just when I think I have torn it in two
It is up in the air and away.
—OLIVER HERFORD

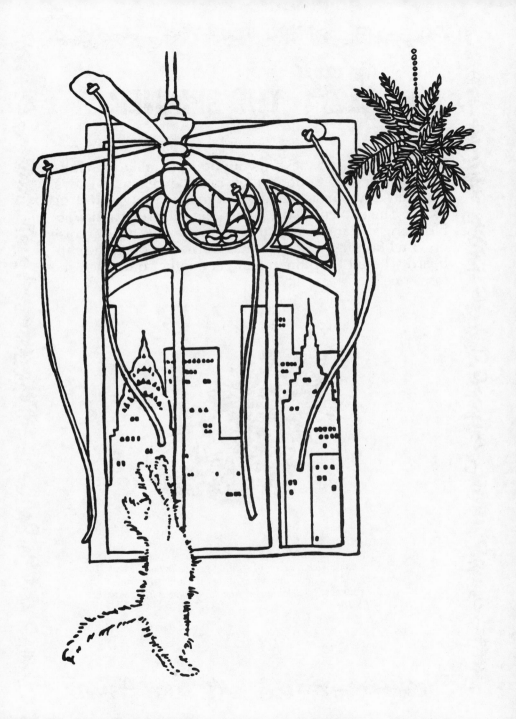

17 THE SPINNER

If you have plastic sticks in your home to make fruit juice ice pops in the summer, they make excellent cat toys. You can buy popsicle makers at most variety and drug stores. The two ends stick out so the stick rolls and wobbles long distances, and the plastic makes a nice noise on vinyl flooring. Little Utz has learned to open the cupboard where I keep them and get another out when she loses one.

Harvey made such a career of stealing golf balls that he had to be moved to a new home miles away from any golf course. In the course of his felonious life he accumulated hundreds of golf balls.

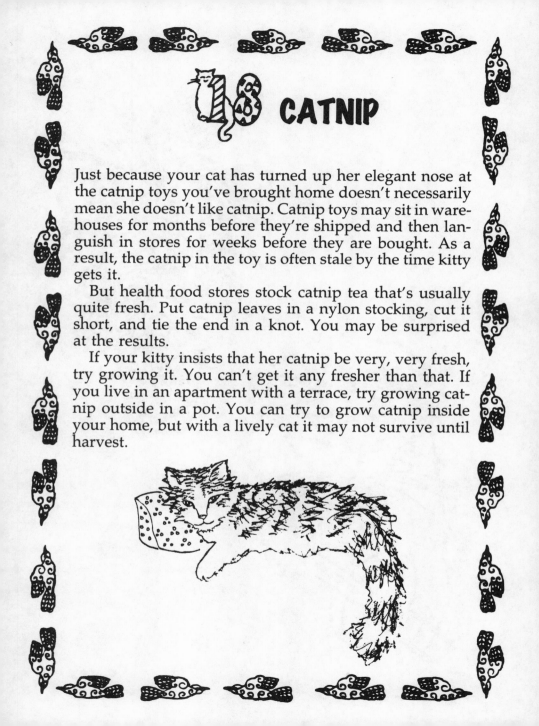

CATNIP

Just because your cat has turned up her elegant nose at the catnip toys you've brought home doesn't necessarily mean she doesn't like catnip. Catnip toys may sit in warehouses for months before they're shipped and then languish in stores for weeks before they are bought. As a result, the catnip in the toy is often stale by the time kitty gets it.

But health food stores stock catnip tea that's usually quite fresh. Put catnip leaves in a nylon stocking, cut it short, and tie the end in a knot. You may be surprised at the results.

If your kitty insists that her catnip be very, very fresh, try growing it. You can't get it any fresher than that. If you live in an apartment with a terrace, try growing catnip outside in a pot. You can try to grow catnip inside your home, but with a lively cat it may not survive until harvest.

A SPECIAL TREAT

Save catnip for days like Mondays or whenever your cat especially misses you. Cats given catnip every day soon tire of it.

In ancient Japan, cats were so esteemed that they were kept on leashes. This practice ended in the early seventeenth century when the government ordered that they be allowed to roam freely in order to kill the vermin which threatened the silk industry.

 **CAT CHIMES**

Make a cross by screwing together two twelve-inch lengths of lathe with a screw eye. Use string to suspend the cross horizontally from any convenient ceiling, staircase, or doorframe. Then simply hang every safe kitty toy you can from various points on the cross, like wind chimes. Use tube-covered strings about two feet long to suspend the toys. Make sure the toys are all safely and securely attached. When kitty attacks one toy, the others dance fascinatingly.

"In the beginning God created man,
but seeing him so feeble,
He gave him the cat."
—WARREN AND FAY ECKSTEIN

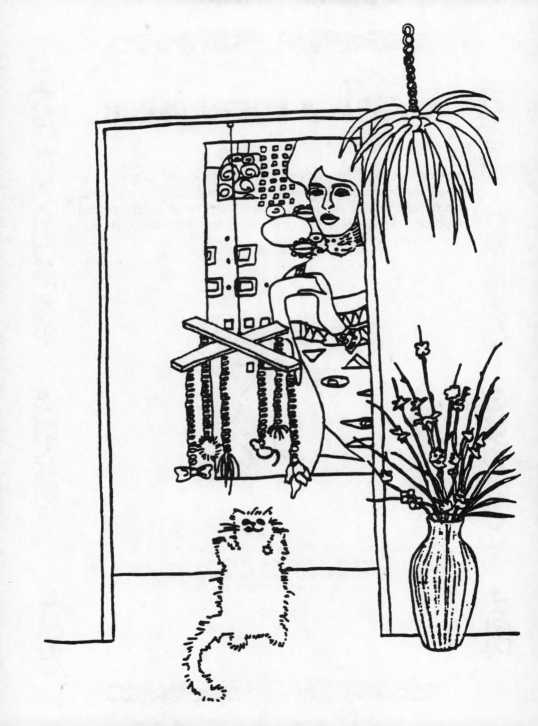

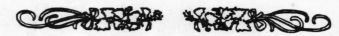

20 A LOFTY PERCH

If your cat likes high places, put a piece of carpeting or a cushion in an elevated spot, such as the top of a kitchen cabinet. Squeak-Butt loves to look down at us from high positions. He feels very lordly and terribly clever that he can go where we cannot.

"Like those great sphinxes lounging through eternity
in noble attitudes upon the desert sand,
they gaze incuriously at nothing, calm and wise."
—CHARLES-PIERRE BAUDELAIRE

21 ROLLER MOUSE

An empty spool of thread with a piece of curly telephone cord through it for a tail makes an intriguing mouse, especially on slick linoleum or vinyl floors, where it rolls with an interesting rattle. Tie knots in the phone cord on either end of the spool to keep the spool from slipping off.

Edward Lear, who wrote "The Owl and the Pussycat," reportedly built his new house as an exact replica of his old one so as not to unduly disturb his cat.

22 HUNTER-GATHERER

Wad paper into balls (not newspaper—it doesn't smell right to a cat) and store them in a plastic bag with catnip. Make sure the bag is out of your cat's reach. Let the bag sit for several days so that the paper balls absorb the catnip smell. Be sure to dispose of the plastic bag safely so it does not attract your cat. Or you can spray the balls with spray catnip. Then place the paper balls in a cardboard box with a "mouse hole" cut out, and present it to your cat for inspection.

You may want to weight the box with a book so your cat can't simply topple it over to get the balls out. If your cat likes to rummage through your drawers, putting the box in a drawer can add excitement.

A GOOD BOUQUET

You can make old toys or wadded paper balls interesting by putting them in a sealed container with catnip. Store for a few days so that the toys absorb the catnip aroma. Your cat will thank you for the extra good smells.

"The animals in the world
exist for their own reasons.
They were not made for humans
any more than black people were made for whites,
or women created for men."
—ALICE WALKER

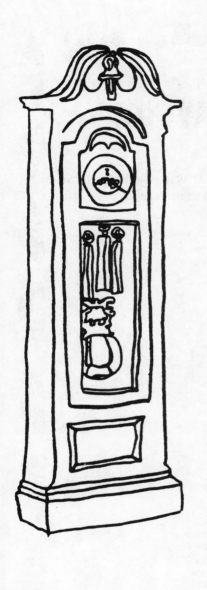

23 PLAYBOX

Cut holes in a wooden box and fill it with balls that can be knocked in or pawed out. Kittens especially love this game.

*"There are people who reshape the world
by force or argument,
but the cat just lives there, dozing,
and the world quietly reshapes itself to suit
his comfort and convenience."*
—ALLEN AND IVY DODD

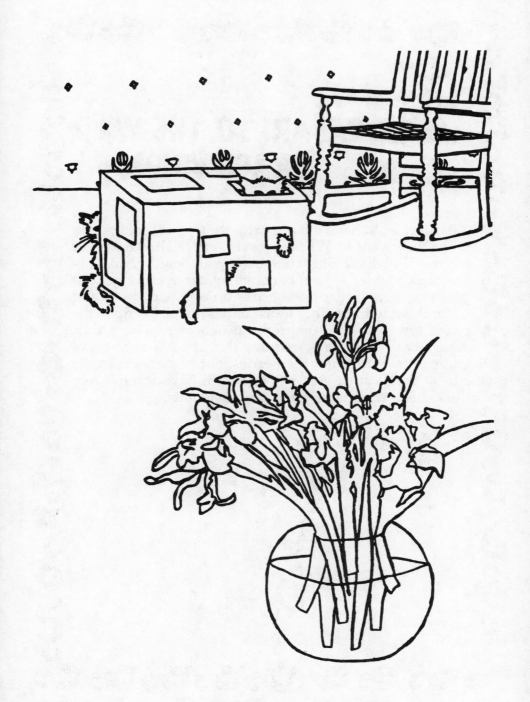

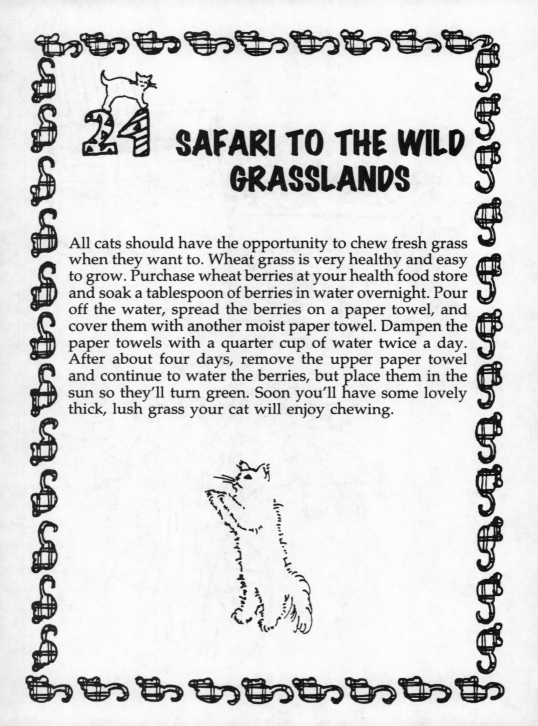

24 SAFARI TO THE WILD GRASSLANDS

All cats should have the opportunity to chew fresh grass when they want to. Wheat grass is very healthy and easy to grow. Purchase wheat berries at your health food store and soak a tablespoon of berries in water overnight. Pour off the water, spread the berries on a paper towel, and cover them with another moist paper towel. Dampen the paper towels with a quarter cup of water twice a day. After about four days, remove the upper paper towel and continue to water the berries, but place them in the sun so they'll turn green. Soon you'll have some lovely thick, lush grass your cat will enjoy chewing.

 # KITTY IN A BASKET

If you don't like the idea of kitty toys all over your floor, then dry out your tub or shower basin and place your cat and her toys inside. The toys make interesting noises on the hard surface. But keep the bathroom door *closed* when you've filled it for a bath, to avoid the risk of your cat jumping into a full tub. Never try this game with a kitten, as a mishap with a full tub would be too dangerous.

> *"The trouble with a kitten is that*
> *Eventually it becomes a cat."*
> —OGDEN NASH

A HUMBLE REPLY TO OGDEN NASH

> *I've often heard it spoken that*
> *The trouble with kits is becoming cats.*
> *I see things another way.*
> *Ogden, hear this view, I pray.*
> *The trouble with kids, for all their faults,*
> *Is that they grow to be adults.*
> —STEPHANIE LALAND

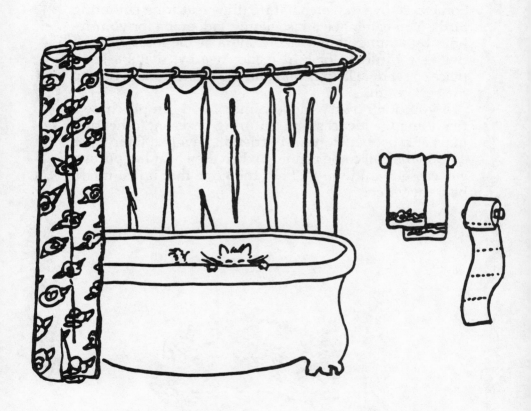

26 TV FOR TABBY

Some cats love to watch nature films featuring chittering birds. You can make a fascinating videotape for your felines by aiming your video camera at the local birds. If there's a birdbath or bird feeder nearby, that's a good place to set up. Use a tripod and the full telephoto setting for best results.

If you don't own a video camera, you can purchase a ready-made videocassette featuring birds and other animals at most pet stores. My friend's cats like their tapes so well they all come running when they hear her putting *any* cassette into the VCR, in the hope that it just might be a cat video.

 **JUNGLE POUNCER**

Cats naturally enjoy balls on strings that dangle very close to the floor. You might want to give your cat a choice of several small balls made of different materials. Some balls clearly have that certain *je ne sais quoi* that felines can't resist. Strips of leather tied together (see Make-Believe Mouse, p. 86) also make a good toy for the end of the string. Stringing up a favorite toy is also a good way to prevent your cat from losing it. Remember to put a tube around the string for safety's sake, and a spring at the top for more fun.

"You can't look at a sleeping cat and be tense."
—JANE PAULEY

LADY CHARLOTTINA'S KITTENS

Lady Charlottina gave birth to four kittens in the woods, and by the time we finally located them they were quite wild.

We now had the task of taming very wild kittens. The first problem was catching them. They had never seen a human in all their young lives and they were terrified of us, spitting and running away when we tried to approach. All sorts of temptations with food failed, as well as our steady cajoling and overtures of friendship. The SPCA told us they had cat traps, but the weight of a kitten was not enough to spring one.

Finally we hit on a plan. We placed Lady Charlottina in a closed box with only a kitten-sized hole cut into the top and an inclined board as a ramp to the hole. Lady Charlottina, trusting soul that she is, never questioned our putting her in a closed box. She purred and meowed throughout the whole experience.

Within twenty minutes each hungry kitten had responded to Charlottina's calls by climbing up the ramp to the top of the box and tumbling through the hole onto the nice soft mommy inside. We then brought the box indoors and carefully placed Mama and her kittens in a large open box full of cushions and padding. Soon the kittens became quite friendly with us. (Lady Charlottina has since been spayed.)

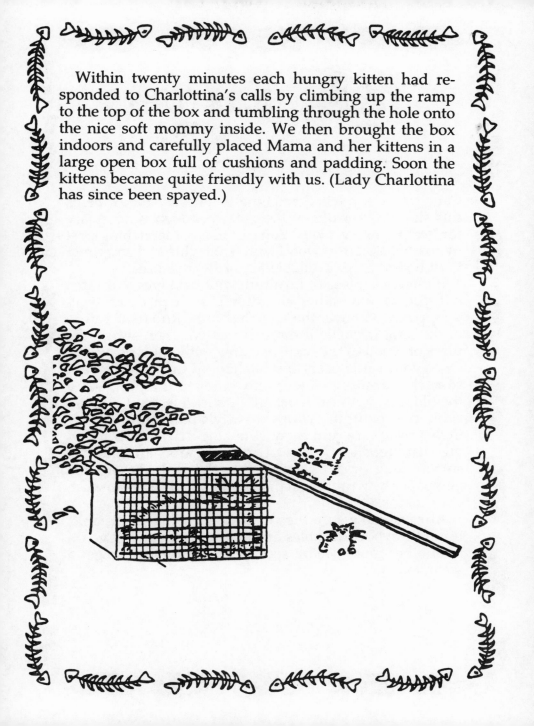

SCRATCHING POST

Cats love to scratch. Scratching is not only fun, it helps cats shed the sheaths of their claws, which is necessary for healthy nail growth. You can make a scratching post by coating a piece of wood with white glue and wrapping it with sisal cord, available at hardware stores.

If there is a piece of furniture your cat loves to scratch but you would rather she didn't, fit a piece of sisal-wrapped wood over the scratched area. Rub fresh catnip in the sisal to make it more attractive. Then secure the piece of wood to the scratched area with more sisal cord. Once your cat is used to scratching at the post, move it from the furniture. After you've moved the post, spray the old area with cat repellent or stick pieces of double-sided tape on it; this clings to Kitty's paws most annoyingly (make sure your cat does not ingest it). When spraying cat repellent, spread newspapers around the surrounding area. When you've finished, discard the newpaper by wrapping it in a plastic bag. Be sure to wash your hands.

Always make sure the scratching post is very stable. If it falls over or wobbles even once, your cat will go on to another more secure spot, and you might not get a second chance.

DON'T DECLAW THAT PAW

You may have heard that it doesn't matter whether or not a cat has his weapons of protection—but it matters to the cat! Many a loving, sweet-tempered family favorite has turned into a terrified, paranoid, miserable creature that had to be put to sleep if only to end his suffering, simply because he had been declawed. Without his natural protection your cat will feel as if he's enacting *Gunfight at the O.K. Corral*, but with blanks in his revolver. A formerly manageable universe becomes hostile and terrifying to the declawed cat. Puss may never actually use his claws but, like a gunfighter in Dodge City, he needs to know he has them. Many veterinarians refuse to perform this amputation. Even if your cat survives psychologically, the operation can cause painful deformities that make him unable to walk without pain or completely cripple him. It is far better to put a slipcover over a chair and use discouraging sprays than to risk seriously hurting a friend.

29 SOFTBALL

A baby's rattle wrapped in surgical gauze or other light-weight material and then wrapped in surgical tape (you can tell I got this one from a veterinarian) makes an entertaining toy. Hang it from a tube-wrapped string. A spring or piece of telephone cord at the top adds bounce.

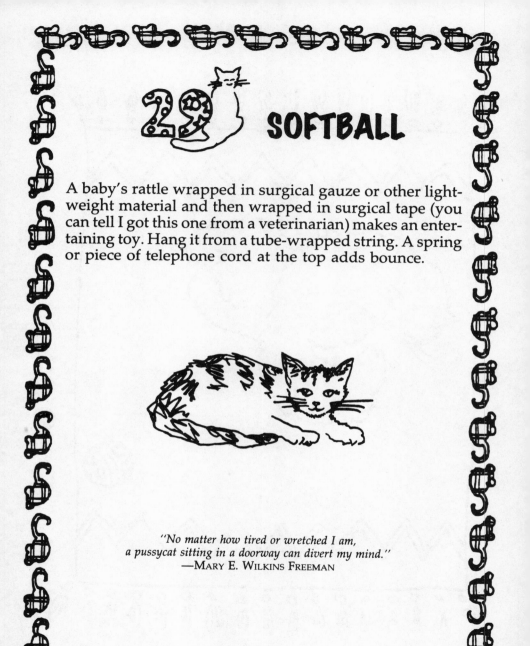

*"No matter how tired or wretched I am,
a pussycat sitting in a doorway can divert my mind."*
—MARY E. WILKINS FREEMAN

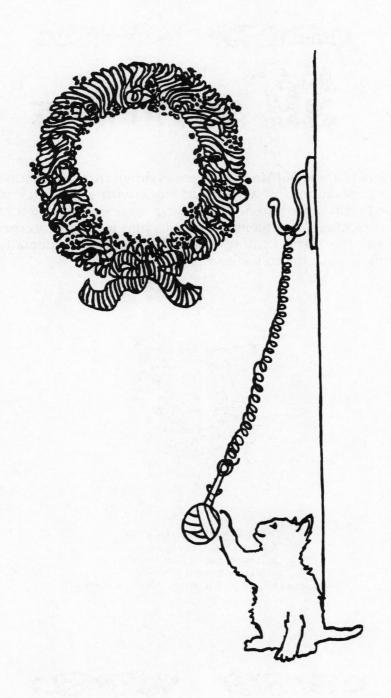

SAFE AT HOME

Here is a fine old standard passed down from generation to generation. Put a wind-up clock with a loud tick in bed with your kitten. The ticking reminds the kitten of his mother's heartbeat and makes him feel more secure. Tape the alarm button down so it cannot accidentally ring if your kitten jostles it.

When human folk at Table Eat
A kitten must not mew for meat
Or Jump to grab it from the Dish
Unless it happens to be Fish.
—OLIVER HERFORD, "THE WHOLE DUTY OF KITTENS"

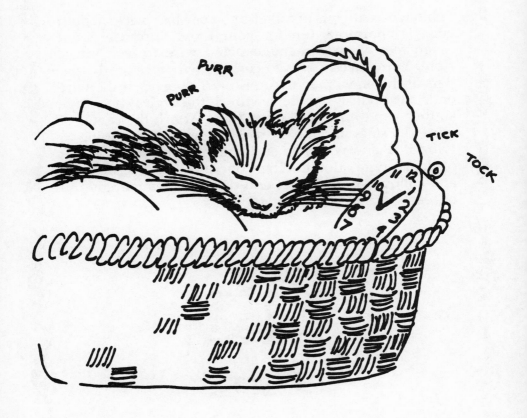

 THE SKITTERER

Piano wire with bits of rolled-up paper-bag pieces at both ends is enormous fun for your kitty. Purchase about seven feet of sixteen-gauge piano wire from a music store. You'll need pliers to curl the wire around the papers at the ends; piano wire is hard to bend. If the wire ends stick out, wrap them with cloth surgical-type tape so they can't hurt you or your cat. Attach the center of wire to a stationary object by bending and wrapping or tying it. Piano wire has an incredible sprong to it that ordinary wires don't. When one end has been caught and conquered, the other end dangles fascinatingly out of reach.

"To err is human, to purr feline."
—ROBERT BYRNE

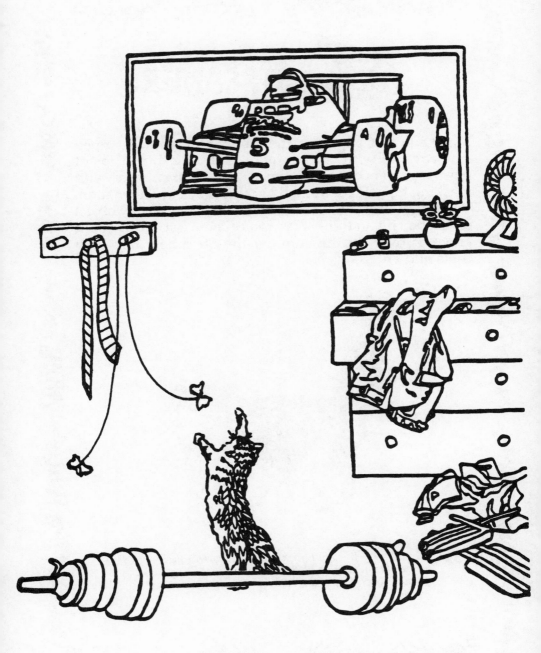

32 STREAMERS

Make a box as shown in the illustration, with one open side covered with chicken wire. Cut long thin strips of newspaper and attach them to the chicken wire with masking tape. Place a small fan in the box and turn it on. You might want to put a dictionary or other heavy object on the box if you think there is any chance your cat might knock it over. In the summer the Streamers box both cools and entertains cats.

During WW II many British families discovered that even before the sirens went off, their cat would sense danger and mew and act disturbed. Their cats made the best air-raid warning systems of all.

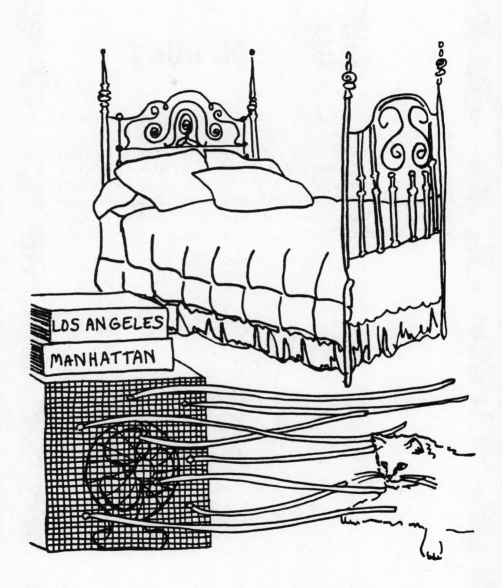

33 EGG HUNT

Put a few beans or pebbles in an empty L'Eggs® brand stockings container and glue it back together. The egg shape rolls in a wobbly way that intrigues cats. You can also use plastic Easter eggs or bottom-weighted roly-poly toys for toddlers. Make sure that the egg is well glued so kitty cannot swallow whatever is inside and that the rattle is too big for your cat to swallow if it does get out. Many cats enjoy these eggs even without a rattle inside.

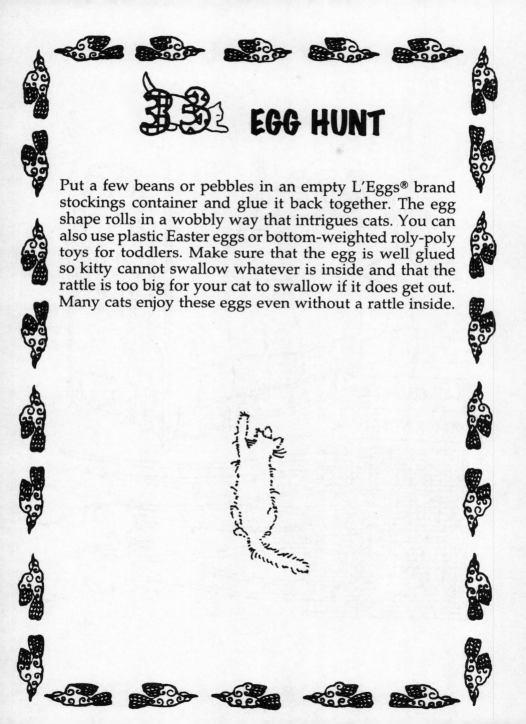

FLYING MOUSE

Attach a length of curly telephone cord across a doorway into which hooks have been embedded. Spray a piece of terrycloth towel with catnip spray and tie it to the telephone cord in a knot. Before you leave, pull on the terrycloth "mouse" and let it spring back so kitty gets the idea.

"Cats are smarter than dogs.
You can't get eight cats to pull a
sled through the snow."
—JEFF VALDEZ

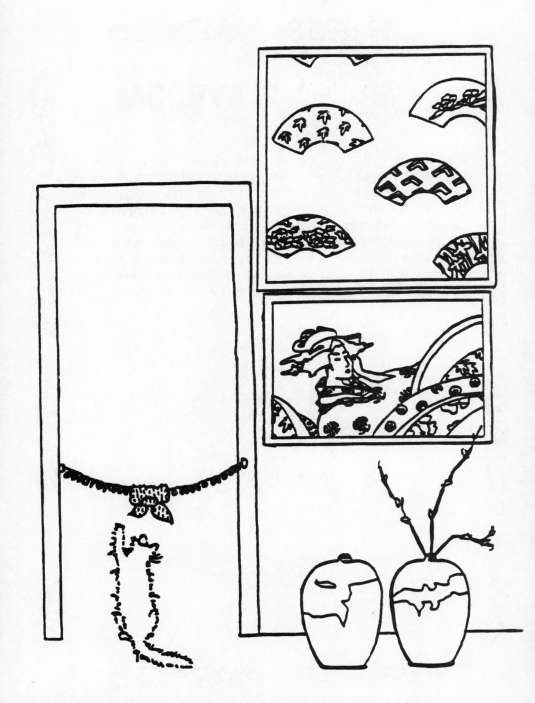

 PLAYROOM

If you don't like finding cat toys all over your home or cringe at the thought of stepping barefoot on a soggy catnip mouse, restrict cat toys to one area, such as the bathroom. Vinyl flooring is preferable to carpeting because toys skitter better on a hard surface. Place a four-by-four wood post (you can paint it to match your bathroom) on the floor across the doorway to keep the toys inside while the door is left open. When you come home you can set the post aside and put away the toys.

"I could half persuade myself that the word felonious is derived from the feline temper."
—ROBERT SOUTHEY

 # THE SQUIGGLE

Tie large, empty thread spools to both ends of a six-inch length of curly telephone cord. Tie knots in the ends of the cord to keep the spools on. This toy wobbles and rattles erratically across the floor, giving your cat a real change of pace.

"Man claims the ownership of earth
Of every glebe and glen
What modest claim do kittens make?
The ownership of men."
—DAVID J. LEVINE

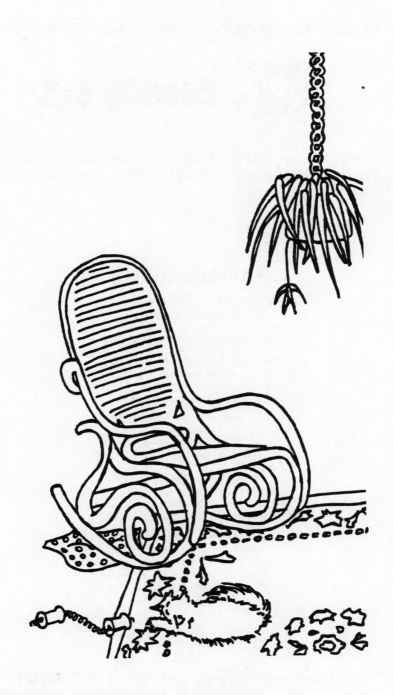

 ROCOCO BIRD

Make a photocopy of this Rococo Bird, cut it out, glue it to a cardboard backing, and dangle it from a tube-wrapped string.

IN DARKEST AFRICA

At evening when the lamp is lit,
The tired Human People sit
And doze, or turn with solemn looks
The speckled pages of their books.

Then I, the Dangerous Kitten, prowl
And in the shadows softly growl,
And roam about the farthest floor
Where Kitten never trod before.

And, crouching in the jungle damp,
I watch the Human Hunter's camp,
Ready to spring with fearful roar
As soon as I shall hear them snore.

And then with stealthy tread I crawl
Into the dark and trackless hall,
Where 'neath the Hat-tree's shadows deep
Umbrellas fold their wings and sleep.

A cuckoo calls — and to their dens
The People climb like frightened hens,
And I'm alone — and no one cares
In darkest Africa — down stairs.
—OLIVER HERFORD

FLIGHT OF FANCY

Use this one only when you're home because it does involve string. Tie a toy to a helium balloon so it just skims over the floor. If two people are home watching TV together they can tap the balloon so that it wafts back and forth between them. Remember to keep tying the string shorter as the balloon loses height.

It is estimated that cats use over one hundred different sounds in their vocalizations while dogs use only about forty.

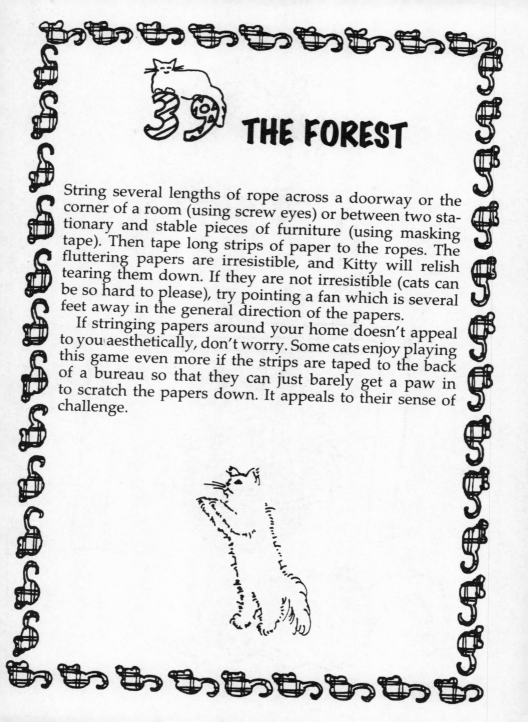

THE FOREST

String several lengths of rope across a doorway or the corner of a room (using screw eyes) or between two stationary and stable pieces of furniture (using masking tape). Then tape long strips of paper to the ropes. The fluttering papers are irresistible, and Kitty will relish tearing them down. If they are not irresistible (cats can be so hard to please), try pointing a fan which is several feet away in the general direction of the papers.

If stringing papers around your home doesn't appeal to you aesthetically, don't worry. Some cats enjoy playing this game even more if the strips are taped to the back of a bureau so that they can just barely get a paw in to scratch the papers down. It appeals to their sense of challenge.

10 MAKE-BELIEVE MOUSE

Tie several strips of leather together into a knot with one extra-long strip for the tail. Cats find this toy very satisfying to bite.

Amber, the mascot cat of my local SPCA, likes to prance upon the key pad of the speakerphone in the office. She sometimes succeeds in dialing real numbers. The SPCA director has returned to her office on several occasions to find Amber breathing intently into the speaker while a jittery voice says "Hello, hello?" So if you get a crank call some night, it might be Amber.

41 PEEPING TOM

Cut a hole in the bottom of a large paper bag. Then tie a wad of paper to a short piece of string and tape the string to a paper bag so that the paper wad dangles in front of the hole as shown. (Soak the string in Tabasco sauce to discourage kitty from swallowing it.) This one can be so much fun to watch you may want to save it for when you're home.

"When my cats aren't happy, I'm not happy.
Not because I care about their mood
but because I know they're just sitting there
thinking up ways to get even."
—PENNY WARD MOSER

SLIDE AND SEEK

A dirt bike tire (16 × 2.125 inches) on its side, with Ping-Pong balls placed in its rim, is an excellent kitten toy. Kittens enjoy knocking the balls around and the balls can't get lost because they stay within the tire.

HOMAGE TO BUBASTIS

The cat has never, I suppose,
Forgot Egypt. His true repose
Now is to dine on cream and cod
And be mistaken for a god.

The cat has never, I would guess,
Forgot the Sphinx. Her best success
While washing cream off paws and bodice
Is being mistaken for a goddess.
—STEPHANIE LALAND

PARTY LINE

Here's one my cats invented while I was talking on the phone. Wrap curly phone cord between some very stable table legs and tie the ends together well. An old washcloth can be tied to the curly cord for added interest.

One day the kitty came to play
And banished all my cares away.
She battled ghost mice in the air
And thus dissolved my every care.

Sweet kitten playing in the dark
Attacking mice that aren't there
What matter cares I thought were real
Your frolics make them disappear.

For what is real and what is false?
My problems or your ghostly prey?
My cares were real until I saw
Your antics made them fly away.
—STEPHANIE LALAND

AQUARIUM TOY

This is a plastic device used in the filtering systems of many aquariums. It wobbles when it rolls. Its size and shape make it easy for kittens to pick up in their mouths, and its lightness makes it easy for them to scoot across the floor.

Kittens, you are very little,
And your kitten bones are brittle,
If you'd grow to Cats respected,
See your play be not neglected.

Smite the Sudden Spool, and spring
Upon the Swift Elusive String,
Thus you learn to catch the wary
Mister Mouse or Miss Canary.

That is how in Foreign Places
Fluffy Cubs with Kitten faces,
Where the mango waves sedately,
Grow to Lions large and stately . . .
—OLIVER HERFORD

 # NEWSPAPER SHREDDER

Roll up about three sheets of newspaper tightly and cut a seven-inch fringe at the bottom. Then pull the inside of the roll down so that the fringe telescopes down. Make a few rolls like this. You can then attach the rolls over a piece of carpet or sisal-wrapped board attached to the wall. Spray the whole thing with spray catnip. Puss will be attracted and scratch at the spot you have chosen.

"Of all animals, he alone attains the Contemplative Life.
He regards the wheel of existence
from without like the Buddha."
—ANDREW LANG

46 WILD KINGDOM

Recordings of birdcalls are available at stores and public libraries. Birdcalls understandably delight cats. I recommend playing them at breakfast; exotic birdcalls provide a wonderful jungle atmosphere.

"There are two means of refuge
from the miseries of life:
music and cats."
—ALBERT SCHWEITZER

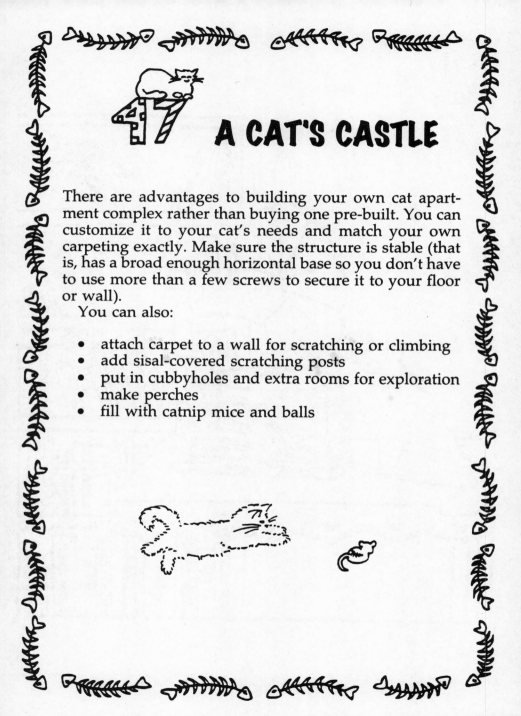

47 A CAT'S CASTLE

There are advantages to building your own cat apartment complex rather than buying one pre-built. You can customize it to your cat's needs and match your own carpeting exactly. Make sure the structure is stable (that is, has a broad enough horizontal base so you don't have to use more than a few screws to secure it to your floor or wall).

You can also:

- attach carpet to a wall for scratching or climbing
- add sisal-covered scratching posts
- put in cubbyholes and extra rooms for exploration
- make perches
- fill with catnip mice and balls

48 PILLOW PAL

Fill a large pillow with lots of catnip for a giant-sized kitty toy.

THE SINGING CAT

It was a little captive cat
Upon a crowded train
His mistress takes him from his box
To ease his fretful pain.

She holds him tight upon her knee
The graceful animal
And all the people look at him
He is so beautiful.

But oh he pricks and oh he prods
and turns upon her knee
Then lifteth up his innocent voice
In plaintive melody.

He lifteth up his innocent voice
He lifteth up, he singeth
And to each human countenance
A smile of grace he bringeth.

He lifteth up his innocent paw
Upon her breast he clingeth
And everybody cries, Behold
The cat, the cat that singeth.

He lifteth up his innocent voice
He lifteth up, he singeth
And all the people warm themselves
In the love his beauty bringeth.
—STEVIE SMITH

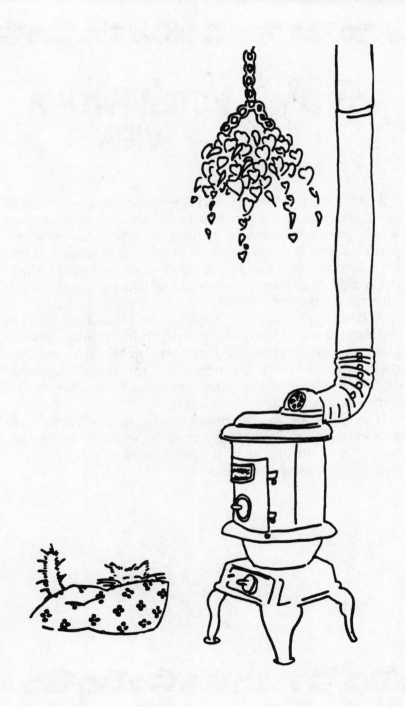

49 ROOM WITH A VIEW

All cats love to look out windows. Mount a secure shelf on a windowsill or move a table under a window for kitty's perch. You might add an outside bird feeder for extra interest if the window is always kept closed. If you feed birds outside at the second story or higher, don't use a dish or anything that could fall; just place the seeds directly on the bird perch.

A hardware store can supply you with film that attaches to the windowpane, transforming it into one-way glass so kitty will not frighten the birds. Also secure a sheet of clear acrylic an inch or so in front of the inside of the window so the birds will not be frightened by kitty's paws scraping the glass.

If you live in an apartment, make sure all your windows are closed or securely screened, even when you are home. An entrancing bird could suddenly fly by, and you don't want your cat to fall.

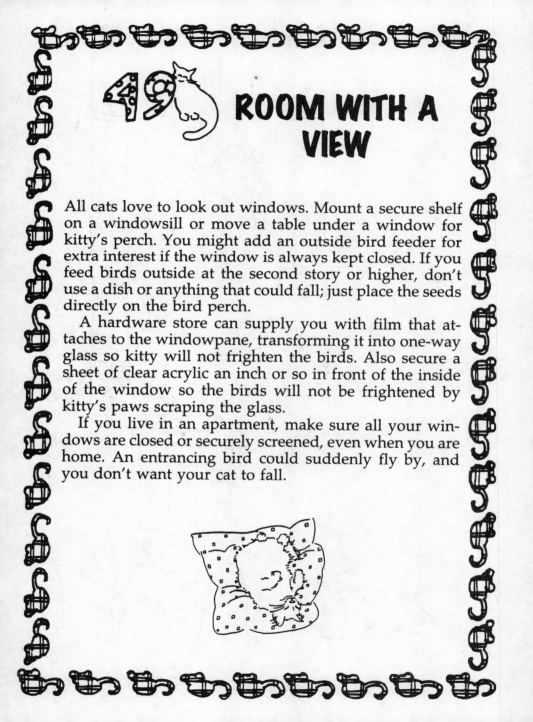

PILLOW TALK

Remember that cats, even in the wild, sleep more than any other animal on earth—two-thirds of their lives. They are also nocturnal, so don't feel guilty if your cat seems to ignore your attempts to induce him to play by himself or if he wants to play with you only in the evening. When you come home at night your cat may be ready for the fun (hunting) to start.

"A dog is a dog, a bird is a bird, and a cat is a person."
—Mugsy Peabody

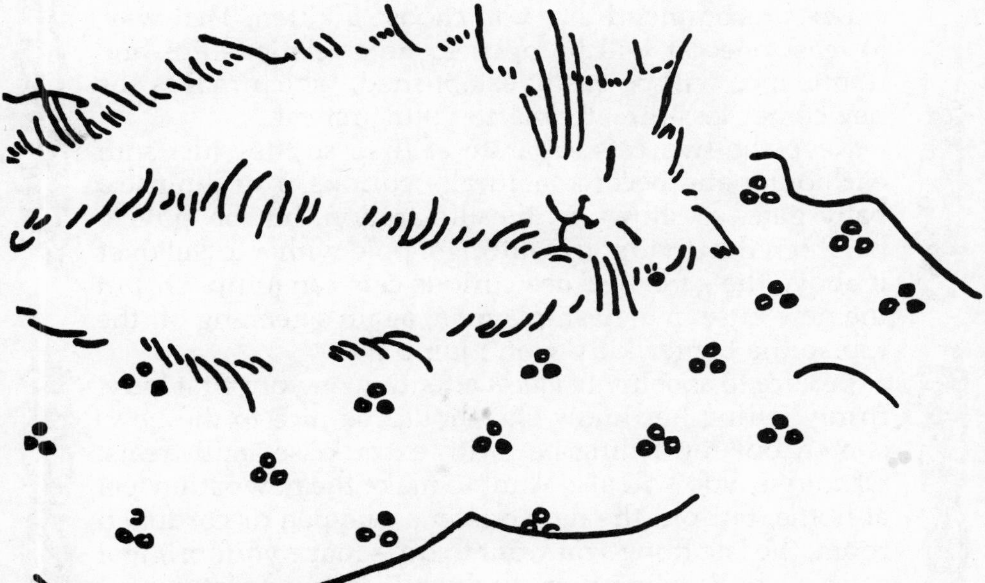

 # THE BEST TOY OF ALL

If you decide to get your cat a companion kitty, many experts recommend that you choose a kitten. That way, at least one cat will be open to new relationships and dominance will be easily established, which makes the newcomer less threatening to your first cat.

Keep the two cats separate at first, so they just sniff each other and become naturally curious. You can use a baby gate, as shown in the illustration, but be sure to heighten the divider by putting a pole with a towel over it above the gate, because curious cats can jump. Or put the new kitty in a mesh playpen, again screening off the top so the bigger kitty won't jump in.

Be sure to absolutely *lavish* attention on your first kitty, firmly letting her know she should be nice to the newcomer, but rewarding her with extra kisses and treats. Of course, you will also want to make the new kitten feel at home, but put the new one in a playpen or cordoned room; the last thing you want to do is make your original cat feel she is being punished while the new cat is free. An old screen door will also work.

A cat will usually accept a new cat of the opposite sex more readily than one of its own. A friend of mine was having no success introducing her new kitten, Polka Dot, to the household until she discovered that bottle feeding Polka Dot left milk-dribbles on her chin which her first cat, Good Boy, liked to lick off. So in a pinch it wouldn't hurt to pour a little cream or canned tuna liquid on the newcomer! And do play games with them both after about a week. Then they will soon learn what fun it is to play together.

Cats do not always cover their litter, especially when a new cat arrives. A dominant cat in the wild will often leave his feces exposed to mark his territory, while other less dominant cats will cover theirs in deference to him. To your cat, you are the dominant animal in your household, so he covers his feces in deference to you. If a new cat is introduced, your first cat may start defecating around the house to establish his dominance over the new cat in a way that the newcomer will understand. Sit down and explain the new situation to your first cat; tell him you love him, and give each cat his own litter box for a while.

"A man has to work so hard so that something
of his personality stays alive.
A tomcat has only to spray
and his presence is there for years on rainy days."
—ALBERT EINSTEIN

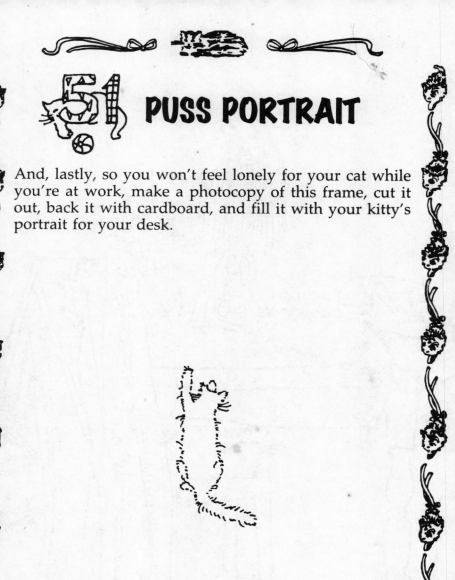

51 PUSS PORTRAIT

And, lastly, so you won't feel lonely for your cat while you're at work, make a photocopy of this frame, cut it out, back it with cardboard, and fill it with your kitty's portrait for your desk.

FOLD HERE AND GLUE

GETTING A NEW CAT

- If you are rarely at home, don't get a single cat—get at least two so they can provide companionship for each other when you're out.
- Do not buy kittens from pet shops that purchase kittens from "catteries." Even if the cats are pure-breds or you want to "rescue" a particular kitten, it's better not to support this cruel business. Kitten farms condemn mother cats to lifetimes of suffering. Talk to your local pet store owners and get to know them. If they know their customers care about the suffering caused by kitten farms, they will make their business reflect that caring. Some farms may be fine, but please don't buy a kitten if you cannot inspect the premises and ask a lot of questions. Also, those pet stores that do care about where kittens come from and how they are treated should be rewarded with your appreciation and continued business.
- SPCA or animal shelter cats are often healthier than those in stores, but they may be euthanized if no home can be found for them. Sometimes cats are given to animal shelters simply because their person is moving and the new landlord doesn't allow cats. Such loving and healthy cats or kittens certainly deserve a chance, so try the shelter first and see if there's a cat there that steals your heart.

- Breeds often originated from nothing more than an aberrant individual that appeared in a litter and was mated back with its mother to promote that aberration. Sometimes this results in breeds with a tendency toward specific health problems, such as the Persian, whose very squashed face may cause lifelong breathing problems.
- Never bring a kitten into a house with toddlers.

SAFETY FIRST

- However cute it may be, don't buy any cat toy that has little eyes, bells, or strings that your cat could chew off and swallow. If you receive such a toy as a gift, be sure to remove the parts that could be bitten off and swallowed. Your cat will never miss them; such trinkets are added to appeal to the human more than the cat anyway.
- If your cat is left alone in a home with a rocking chair, remember to put a pillow under the rocker to prevent pinched tails or paws.
- As I've mentioned before, I strongly advise against leaving a cat alone with a string toy. When I first started researching this book, I called many veterinarians for their input. I thought at first they were being overcautious, but soon found that many had had similar experiences having to operate on cats to remove string from their intestines. One vet had even pulled an electric cord *including the plug* from one particularly gluttonous cat's stomach! So please: no strings. And if your cat seems to have a liking for electrical wiring and chews on it when you're not at home, try smearing the wire with Tabasco sauce.

- If you have a kitten, keep the toilet lid closed to prevent drowning. Also keep the dryer door closed at all times. If you find Kitten snuggled up in this warm and cozy place, just close the door and bang on it loudly with pots and pans. Kitten *won't* go back. This also works for ovens and refrigerators.
- Eaten Christmas tinsel can slice into a cat's intestines. Use other, safer ornaments.

HELPFUL HINTS

- How do you dissuade a lively cat from doing something you don't want it to do? (Good luck.) Try talking to it in Felinese. When mama cats are annoyed by little ones, they growl and the kittens understand perfectly. So rather than saying "No," you might try softly growling at your cat. Hissing escalates the message when appropriate.
- Some cats are allergic to plastic. If you notice a reaction or if your cat doesn't seem to want to drink enough liquid, try ceramic or glass bowls.
- There are great products on the market for eliminating the smell of cat urine. When sprayed on a urine spot, these products actually change the chemical makeup of the urine to another substance that has no odor, so they are not just a cover-up. You can also buy a black light that makes urine spots glow in the dark, so you can find them to spray with the neutralizer. Ask for these products at your pet store.

- You can "just say no" to furs by not buying those cute-looking toys made of real fur. Your kitty can have lots of fun without contributing to another poor creature's misery. Better yet, if you're wondering what to do with that old outdated fur coat, why not cut it up and make your own fur toys and distribute them to your friends with cats?
- Forty-five cats are born for every person in the United States. This is an emergency and unwanted animals are suffering. Please don't hesitate—SPAY or NEUTER! Don't even consider having your children witness the miracle of feline birth unless you are willing to teach them to take full responsibility for their actions and witness the misery of death. Forty-five cats for each person is far too many. Give a shelter cat a second chance, but don't add five more to the gas chambers.

And They Lived Happily Ever After!